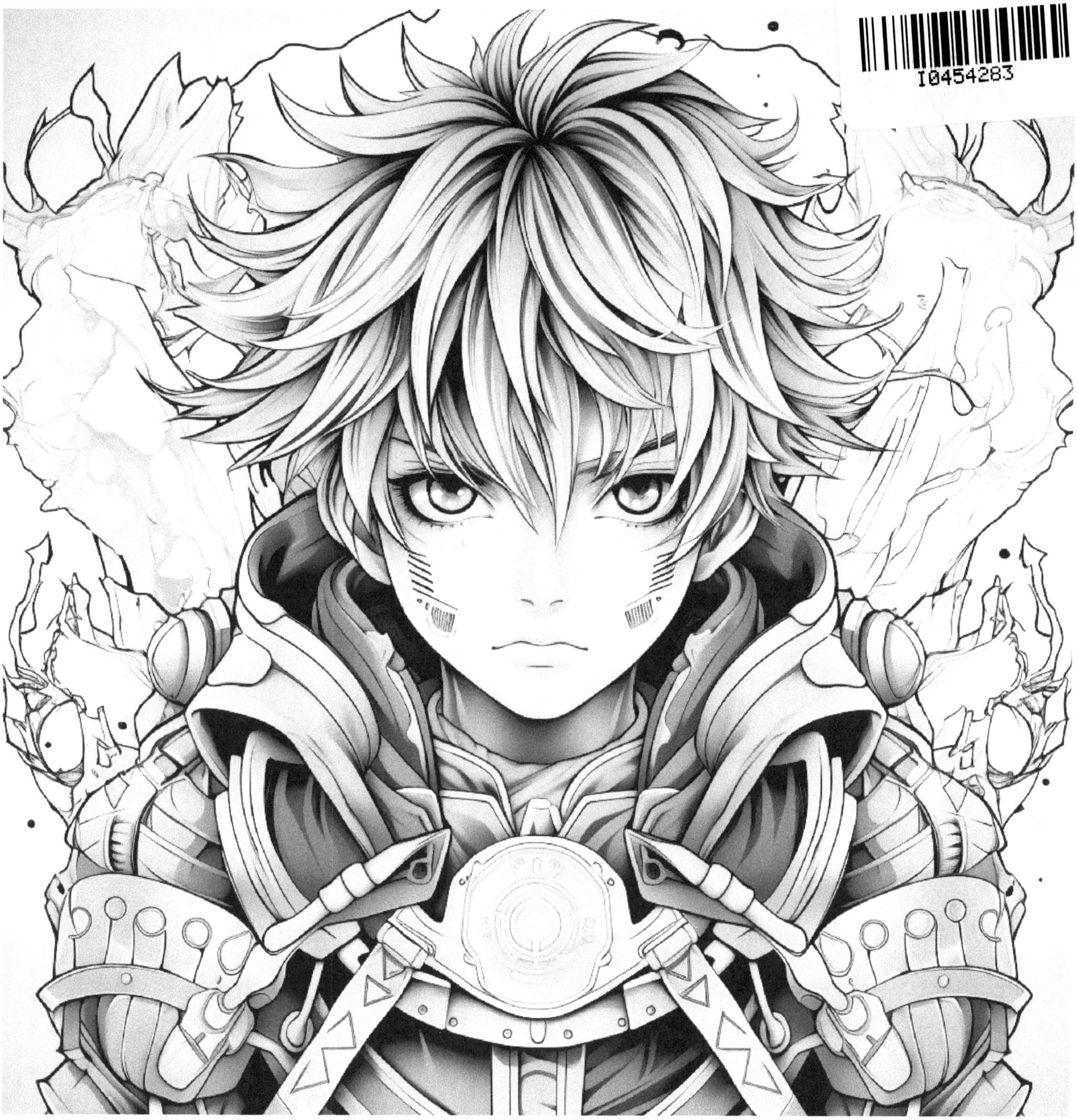

THIS COLORING BOOK
BELONGS TO:

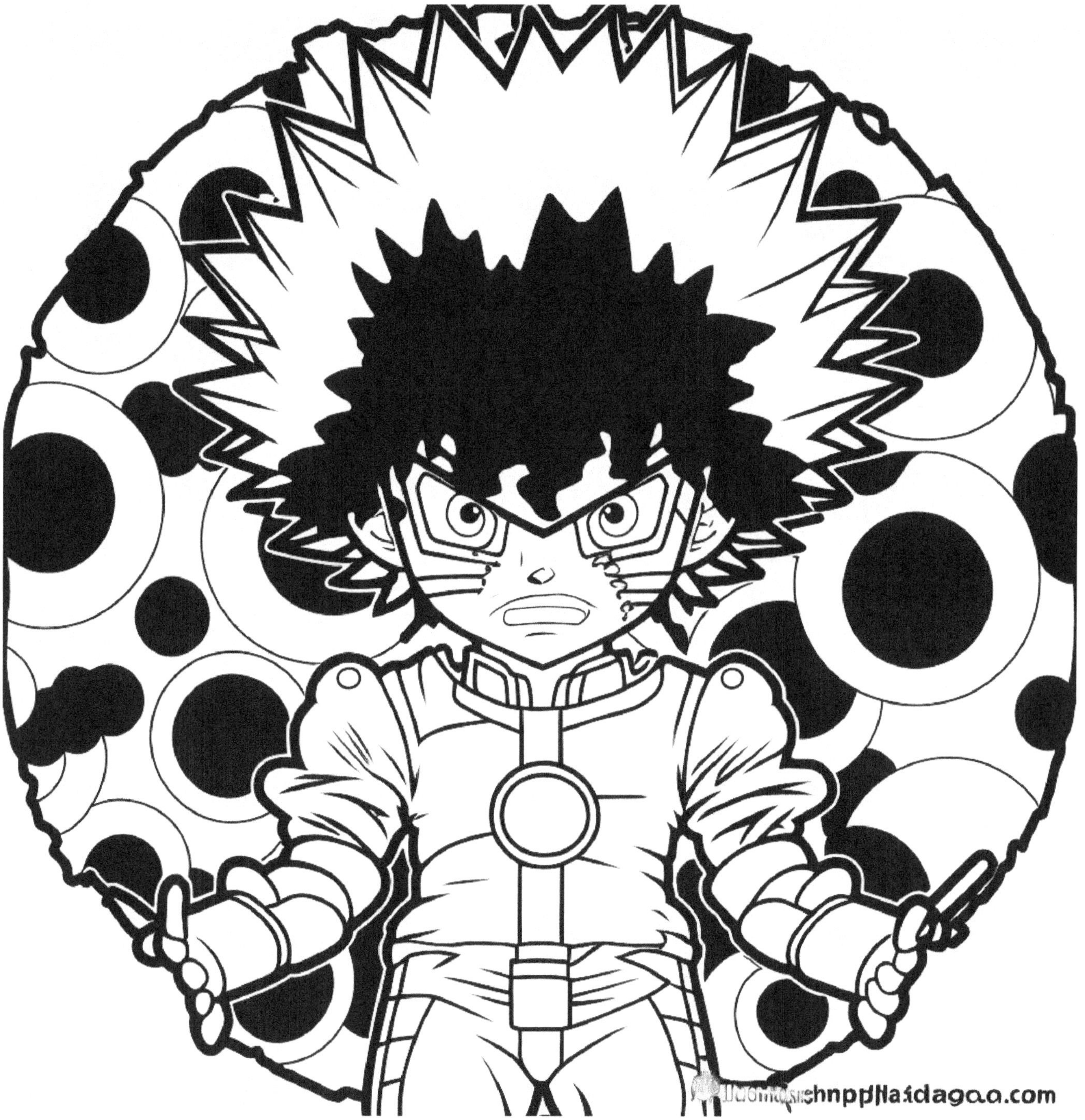

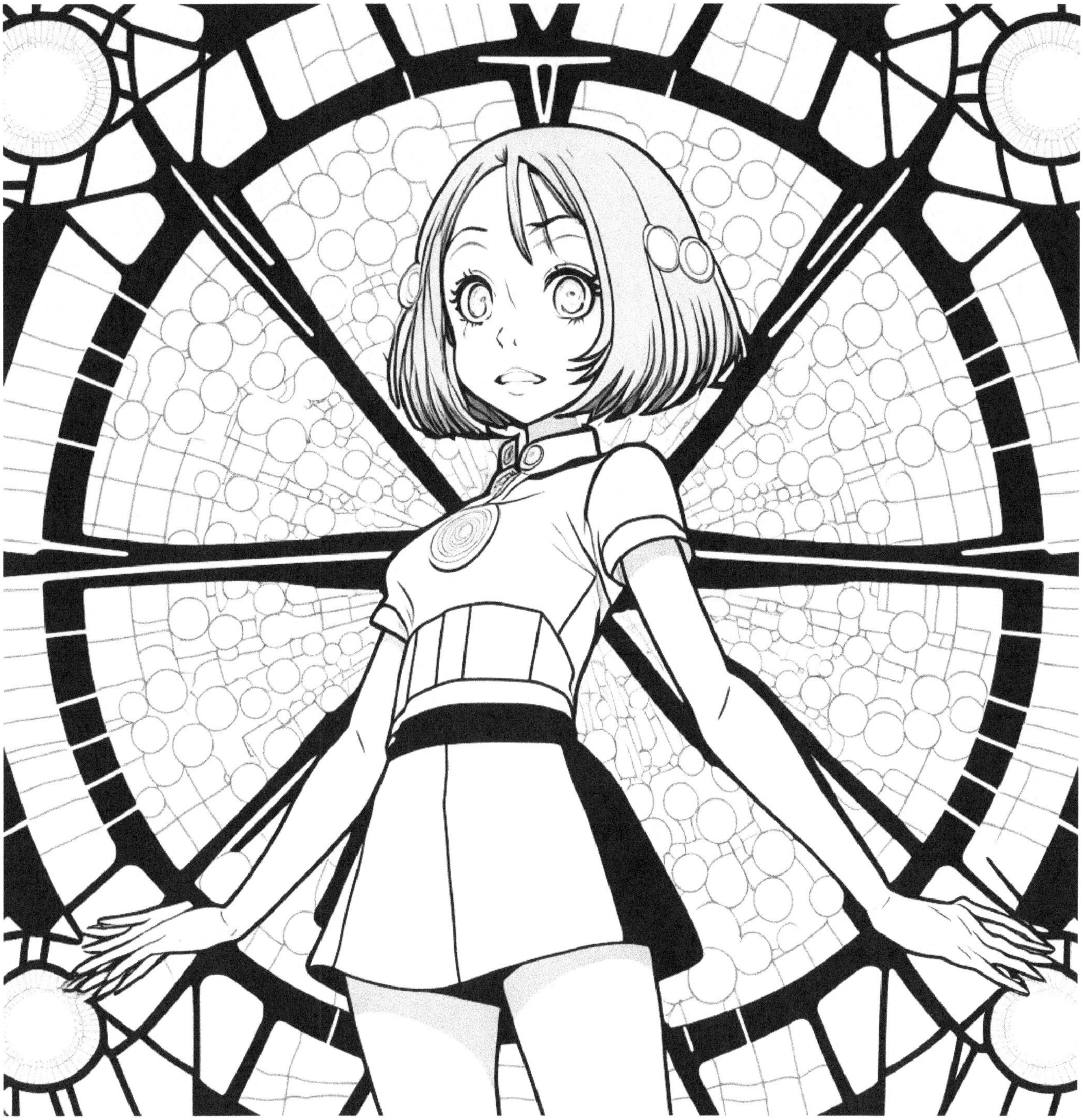

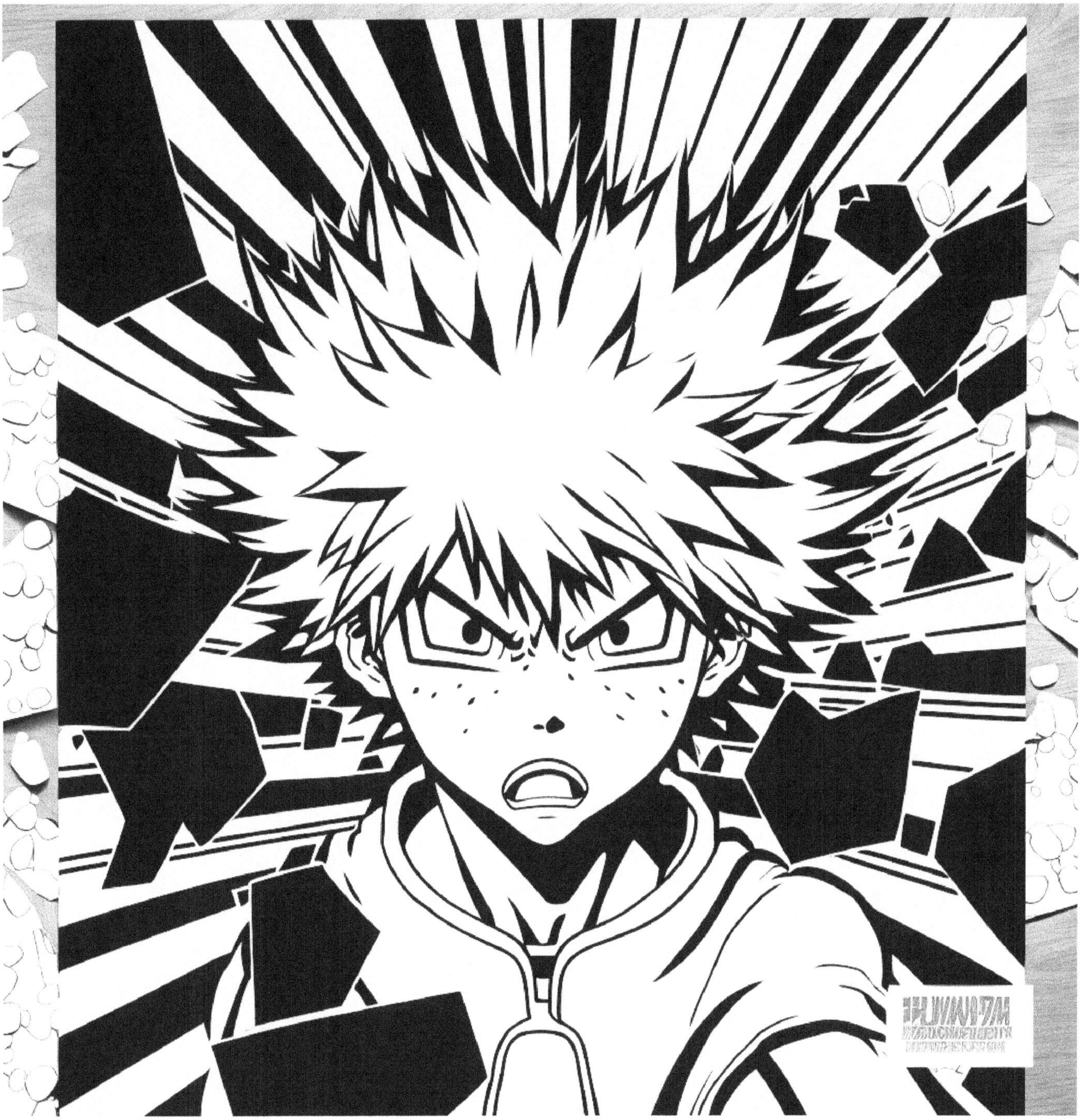

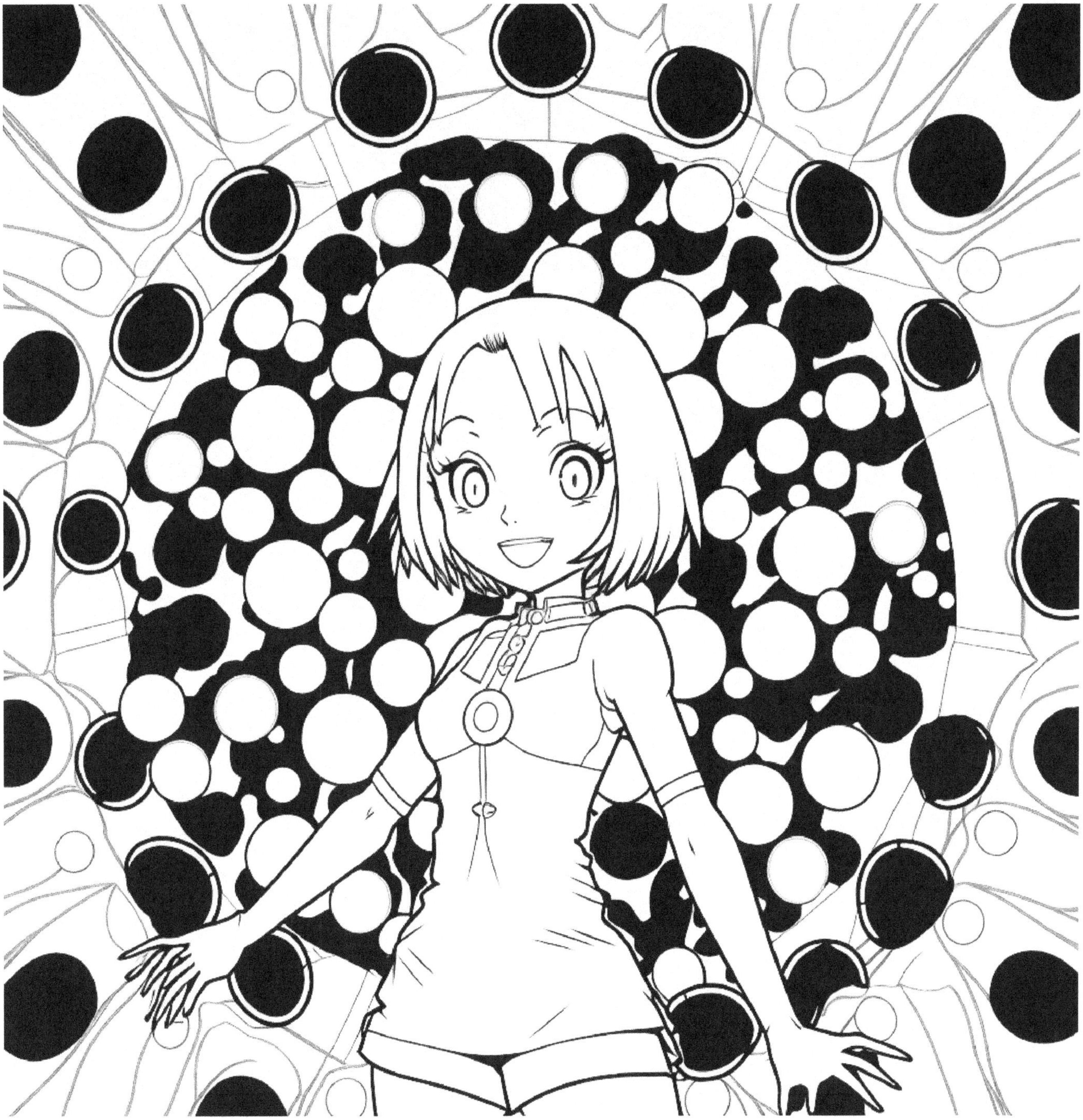

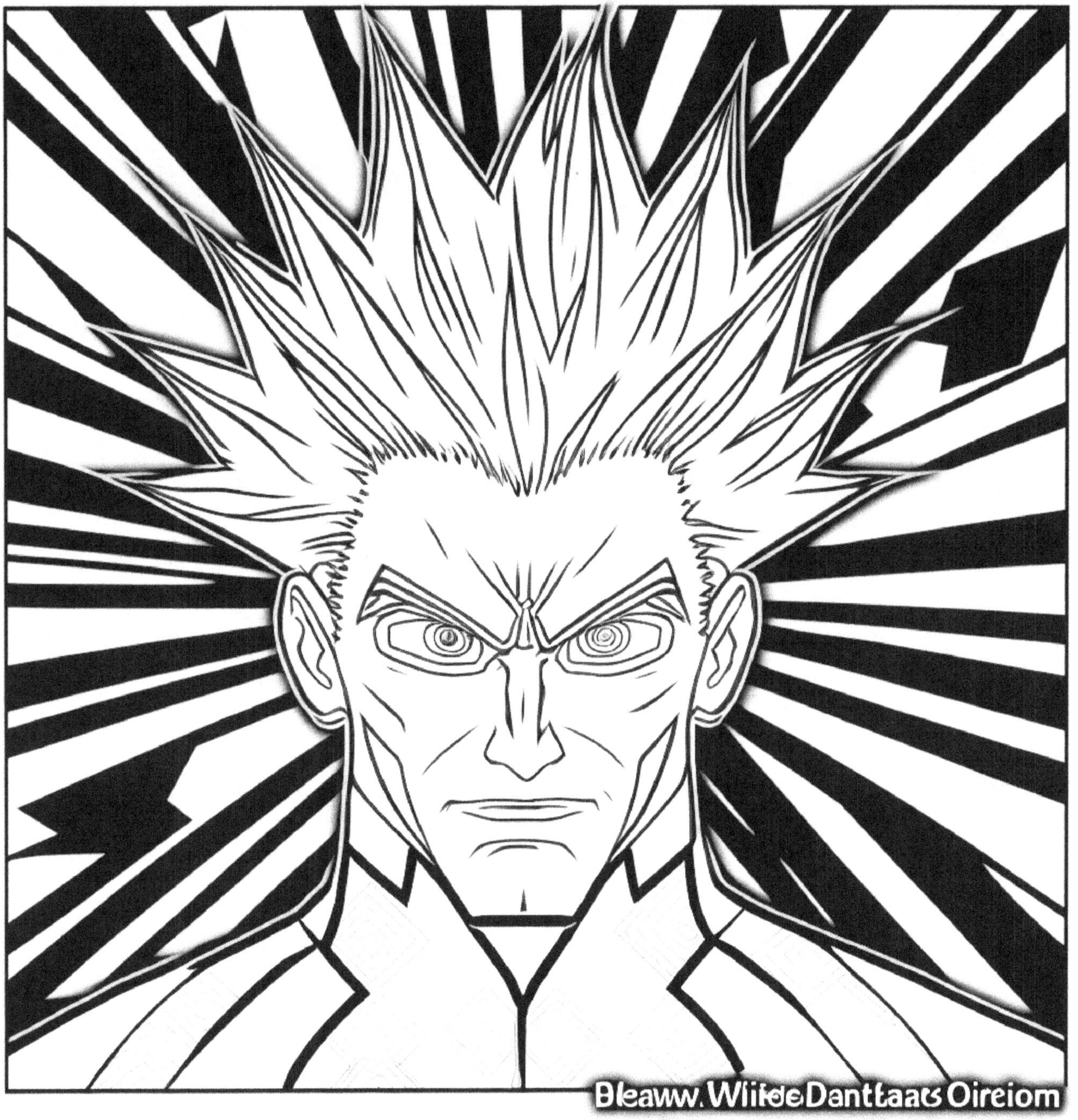
Bleaww. Wiifde Danttaats Oireiom

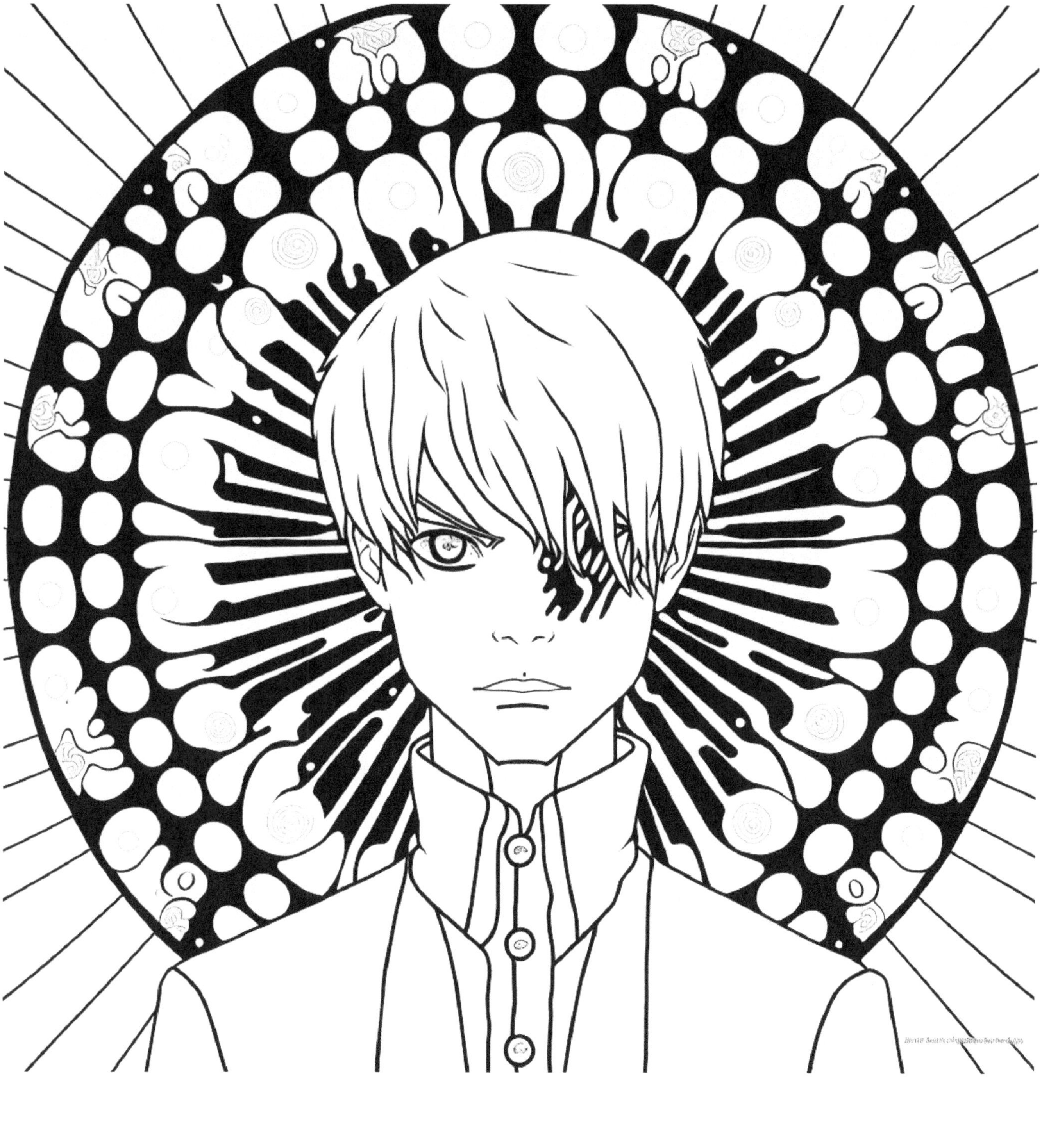

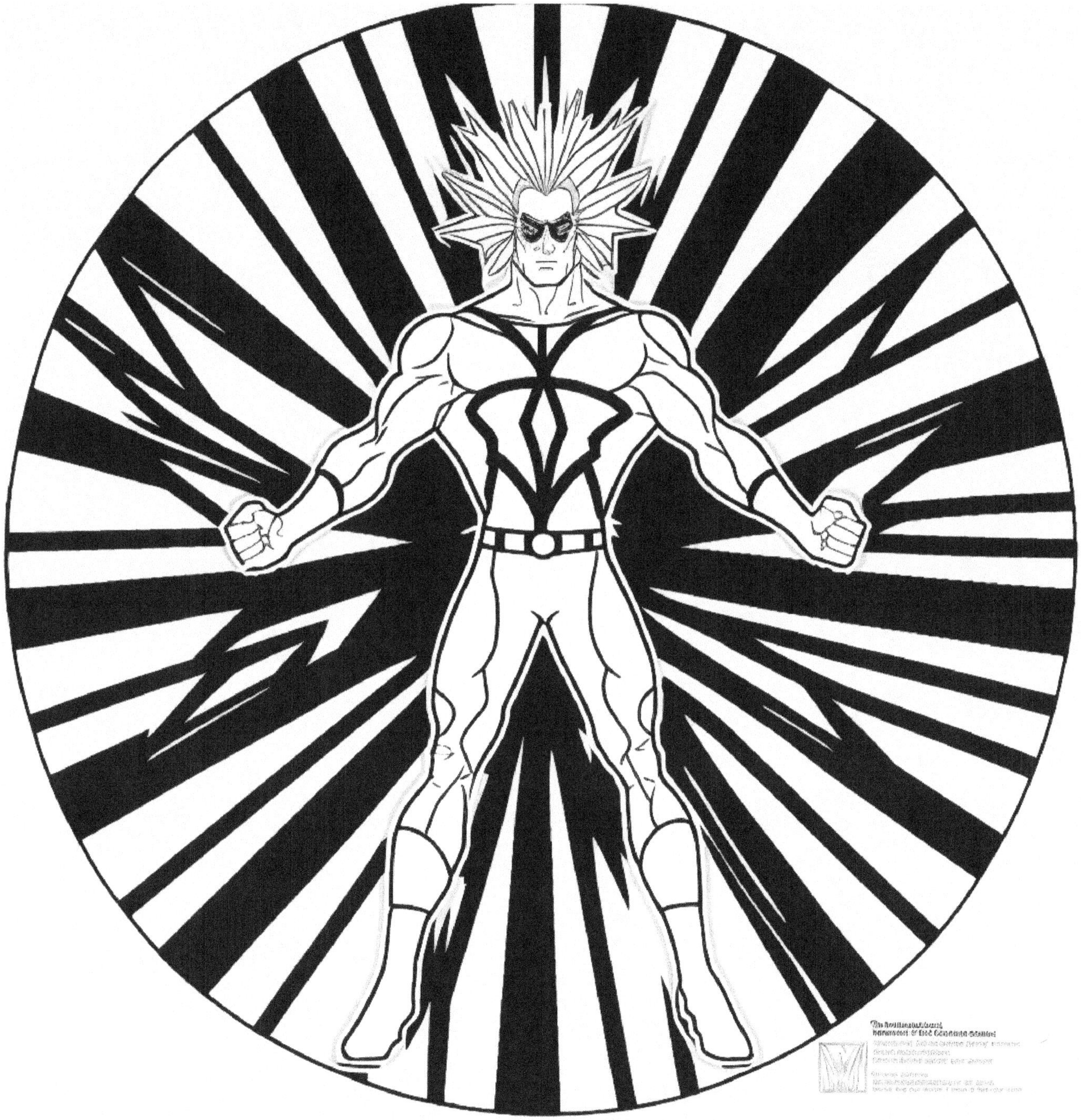

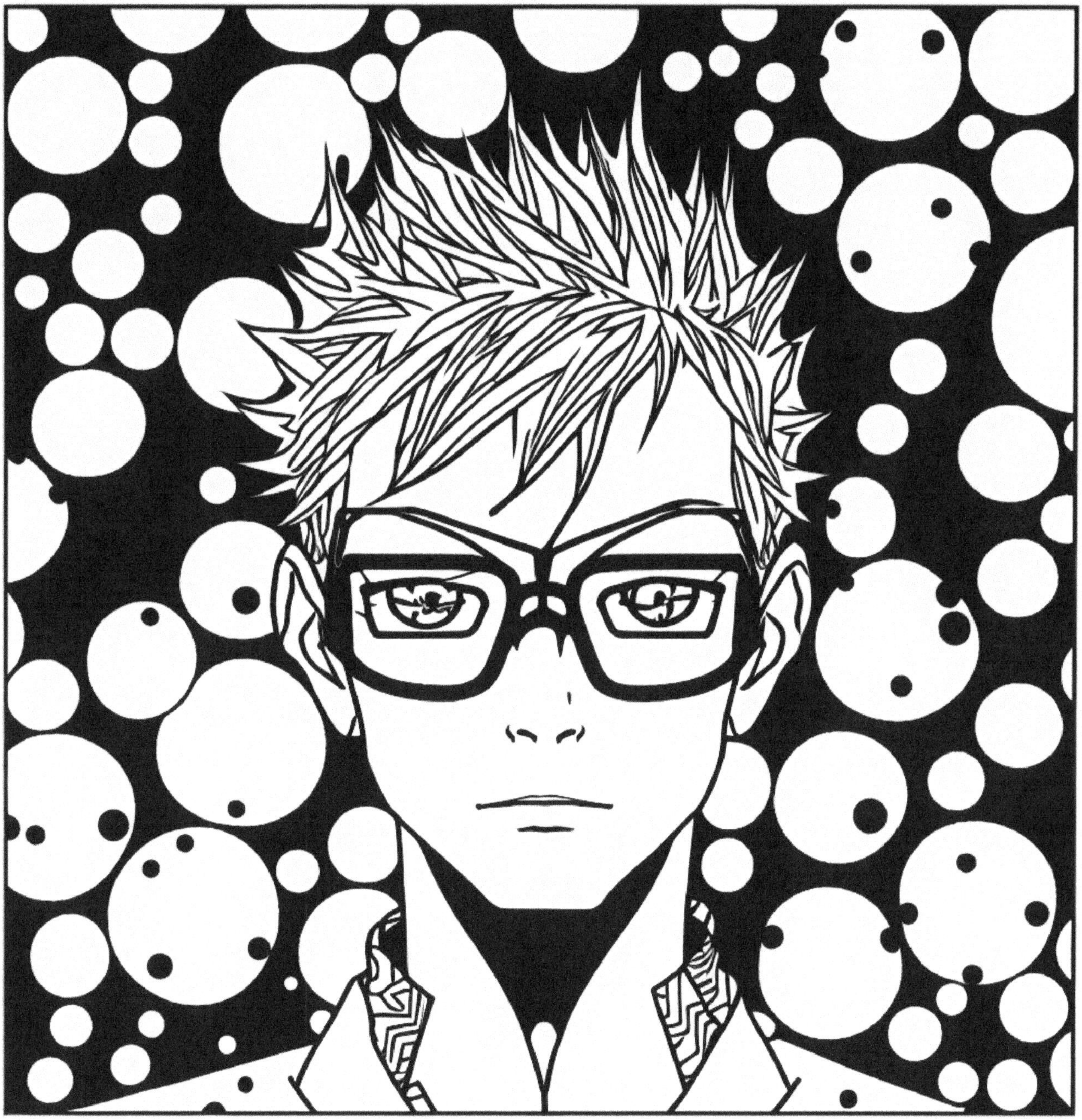

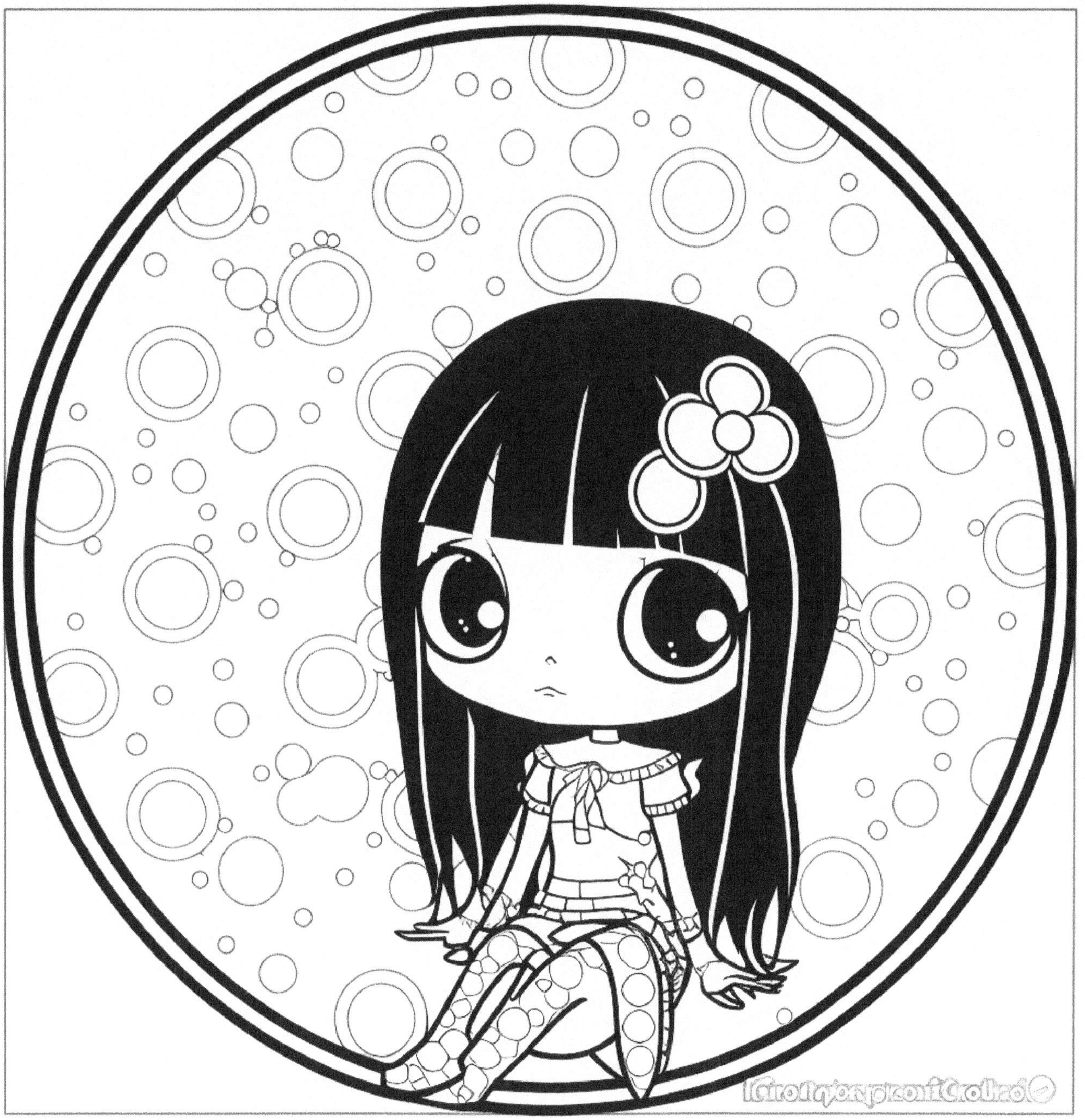

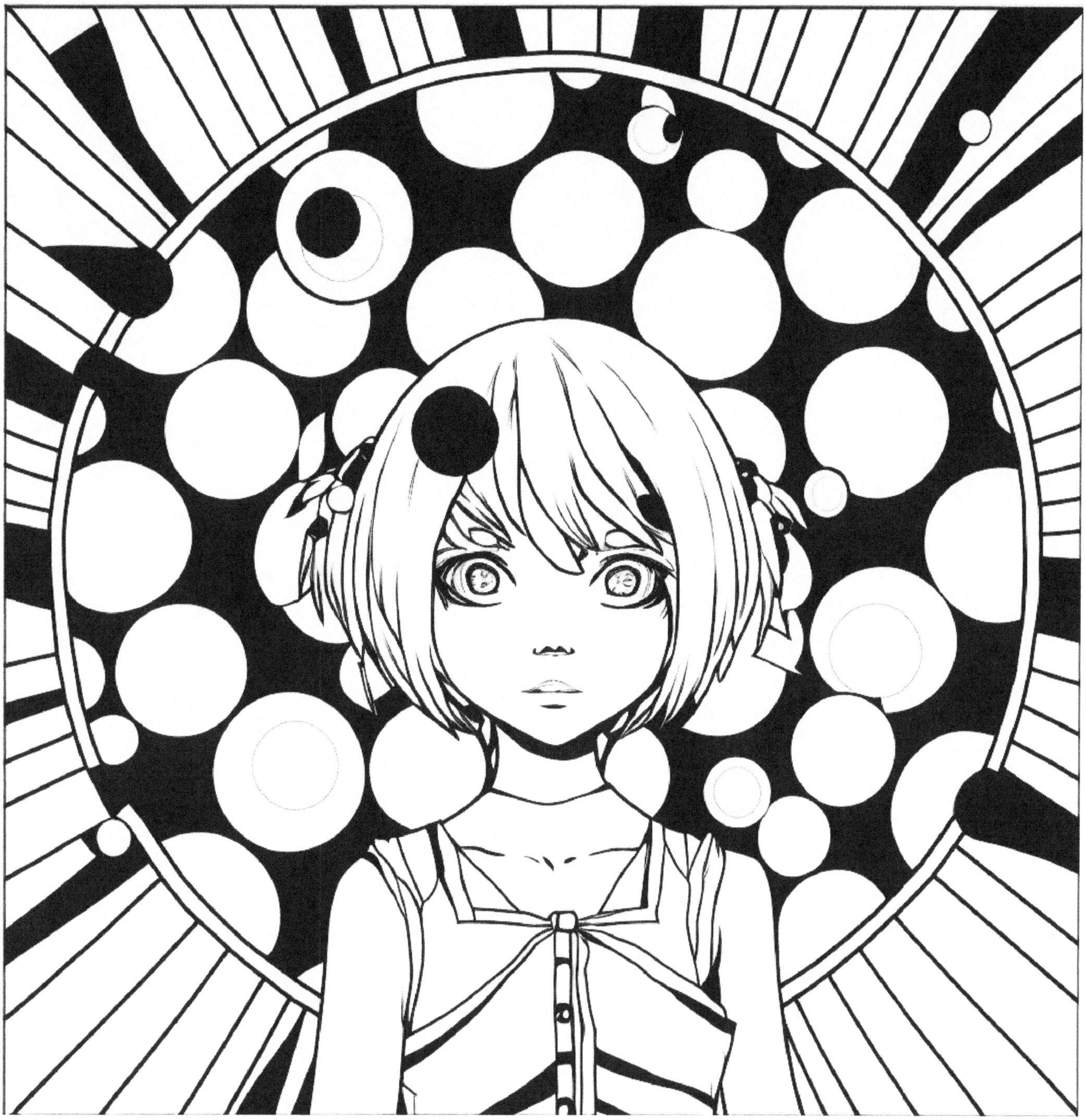

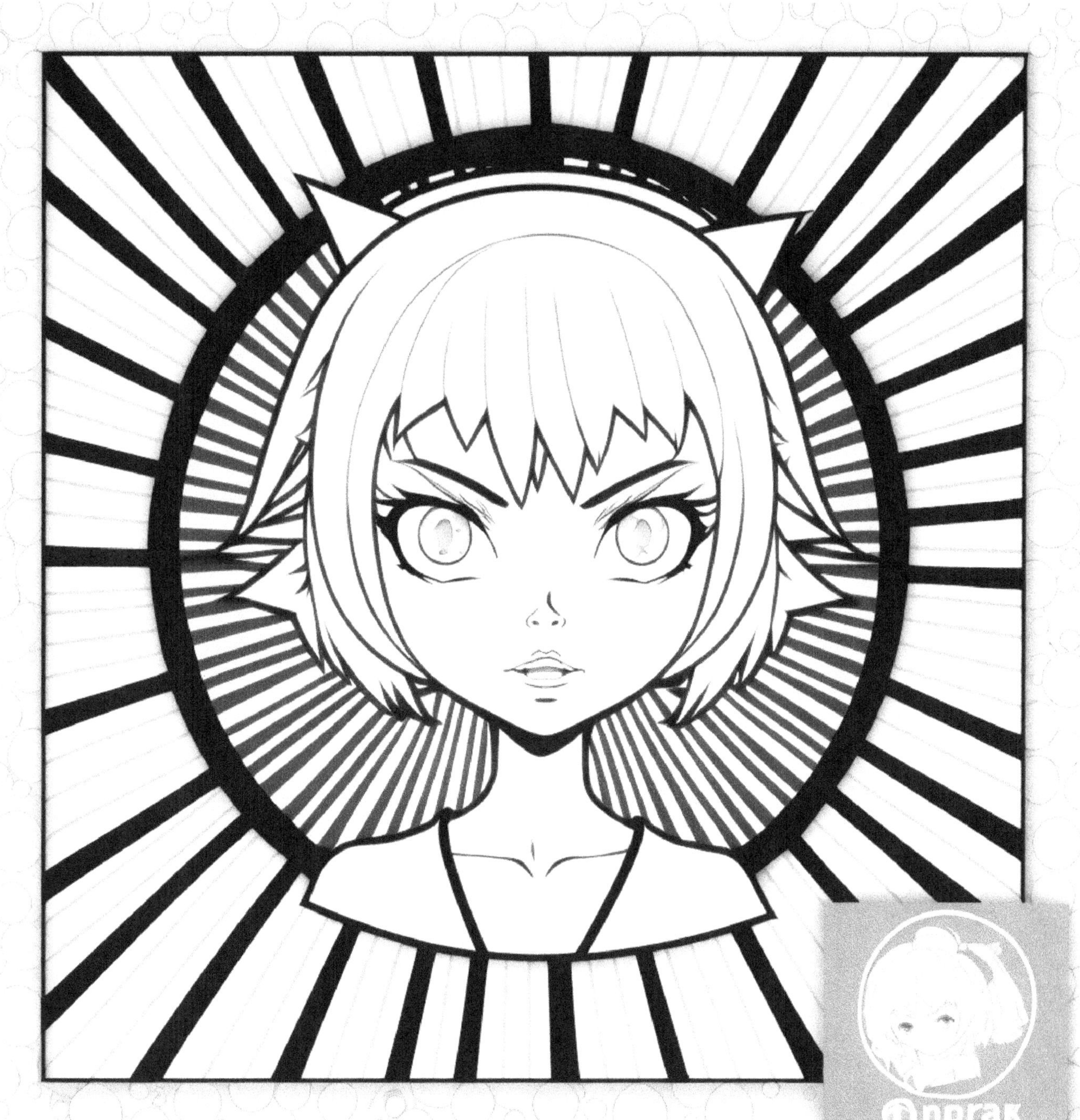

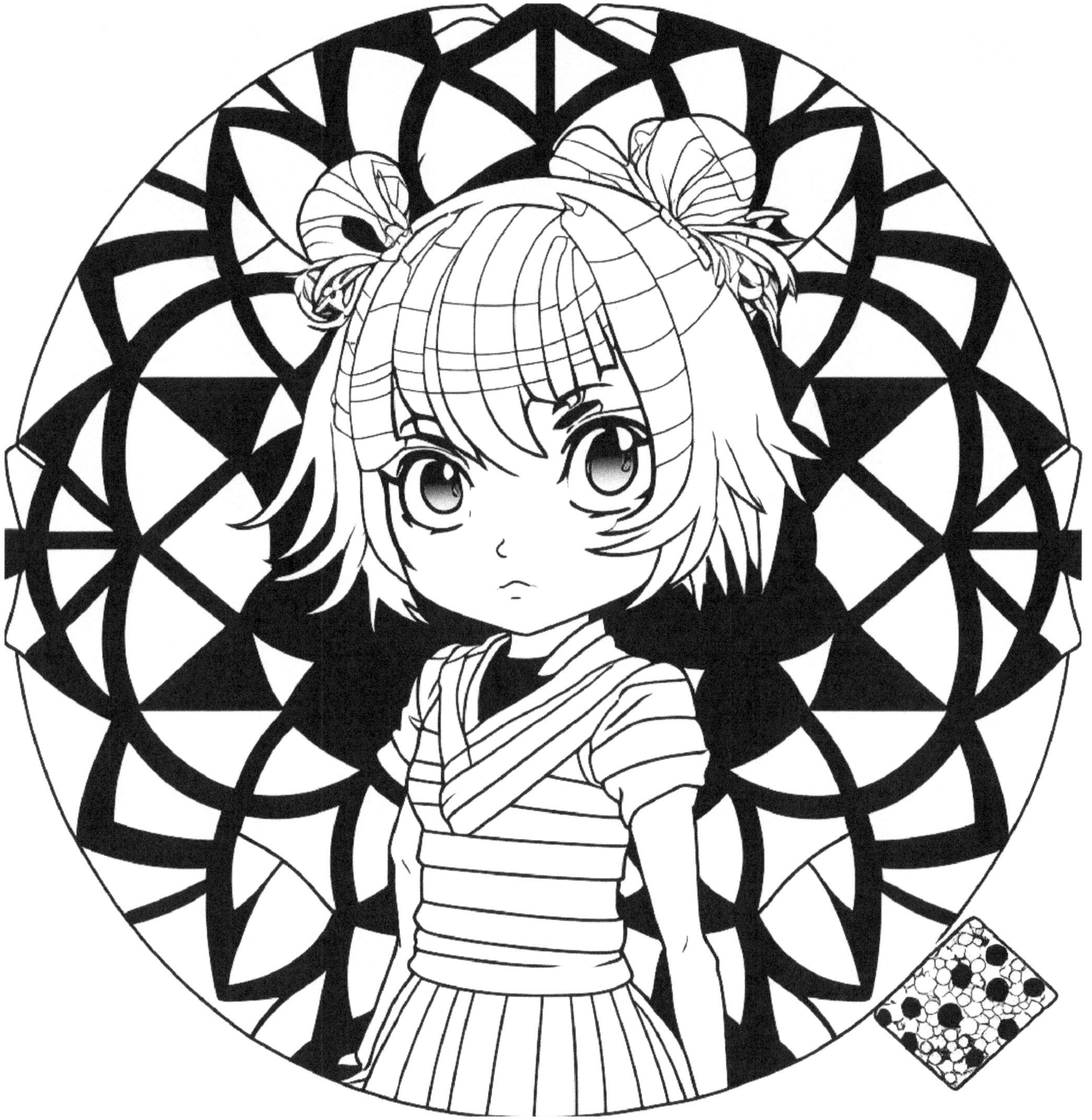

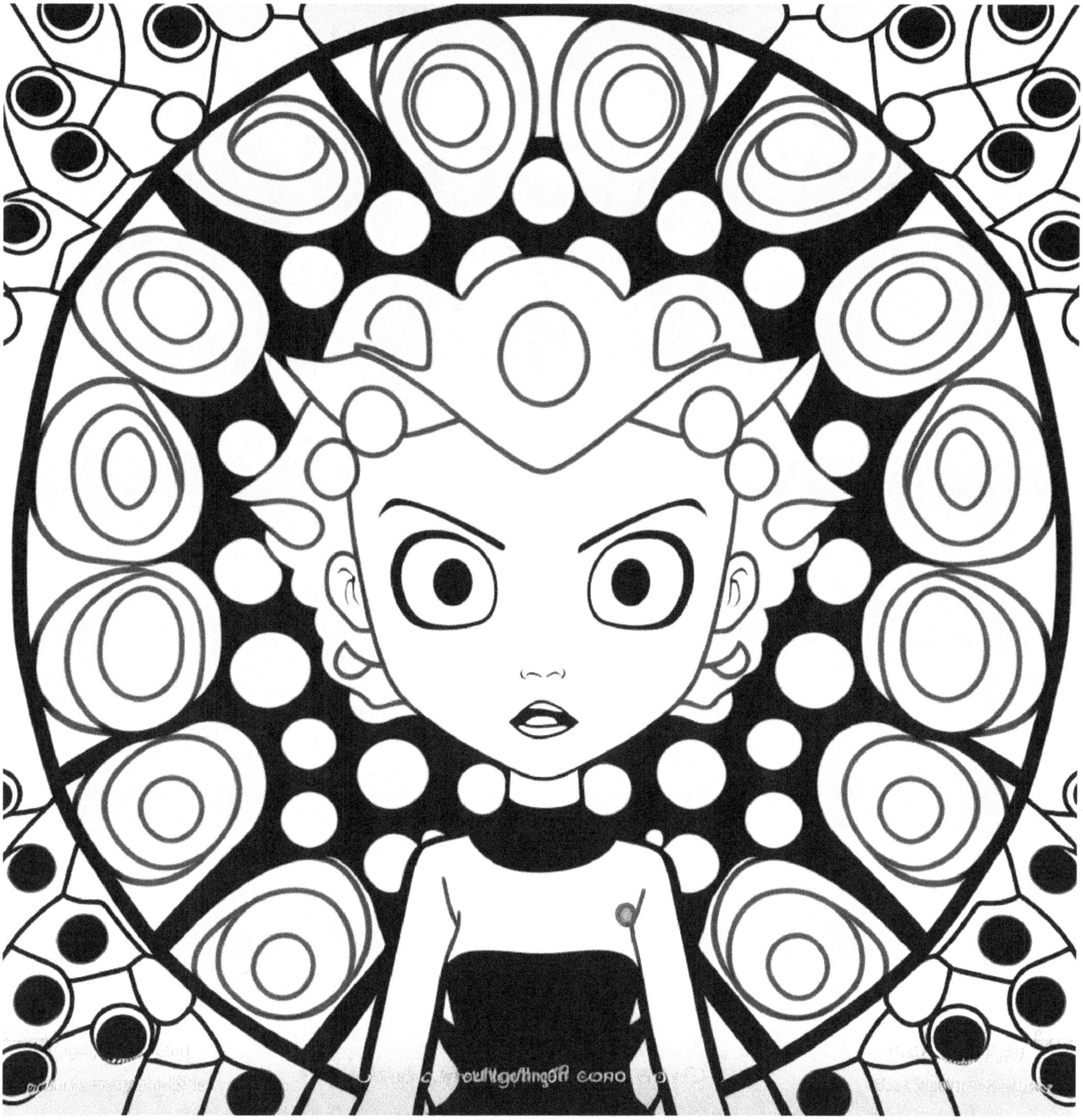

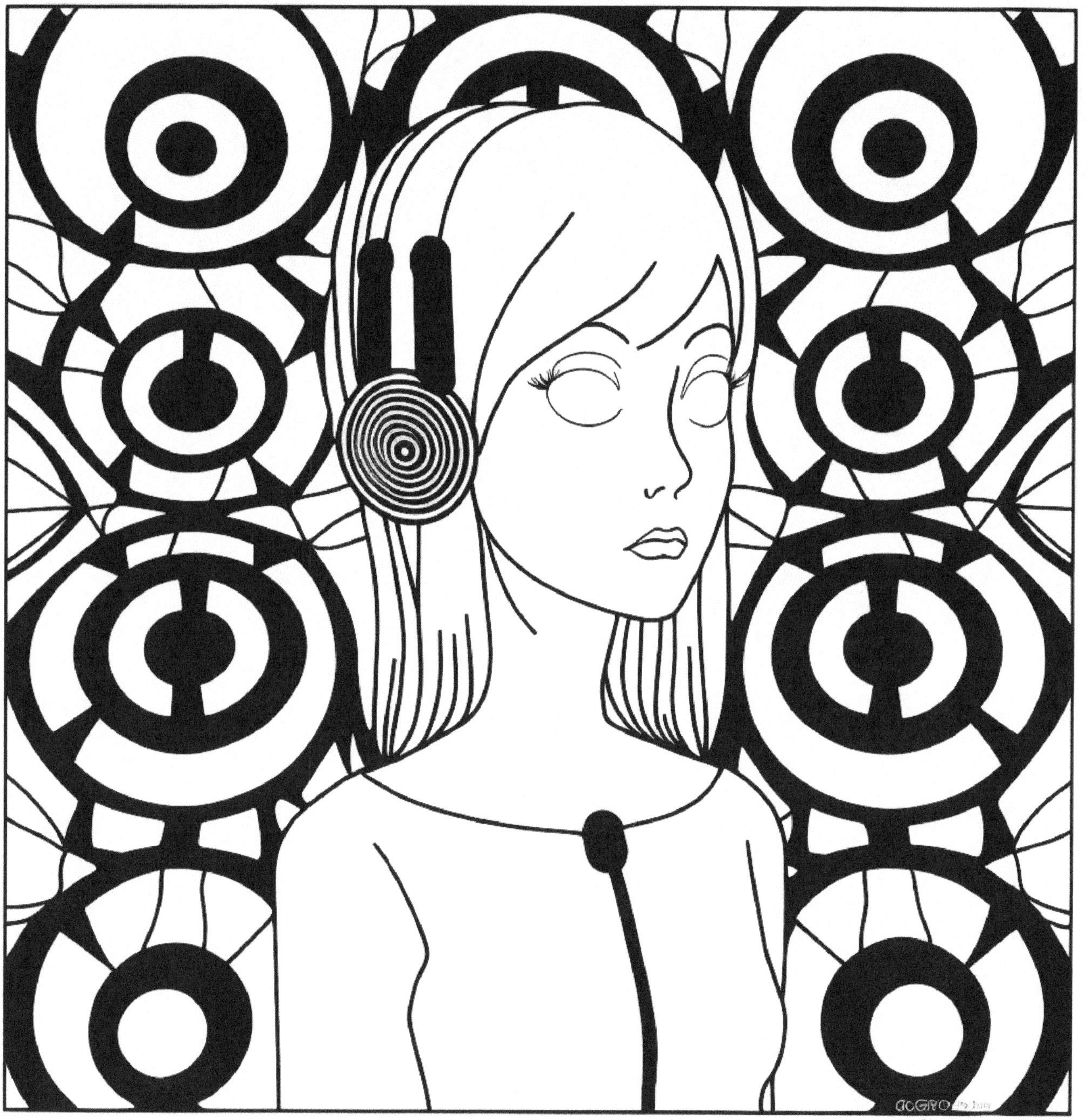

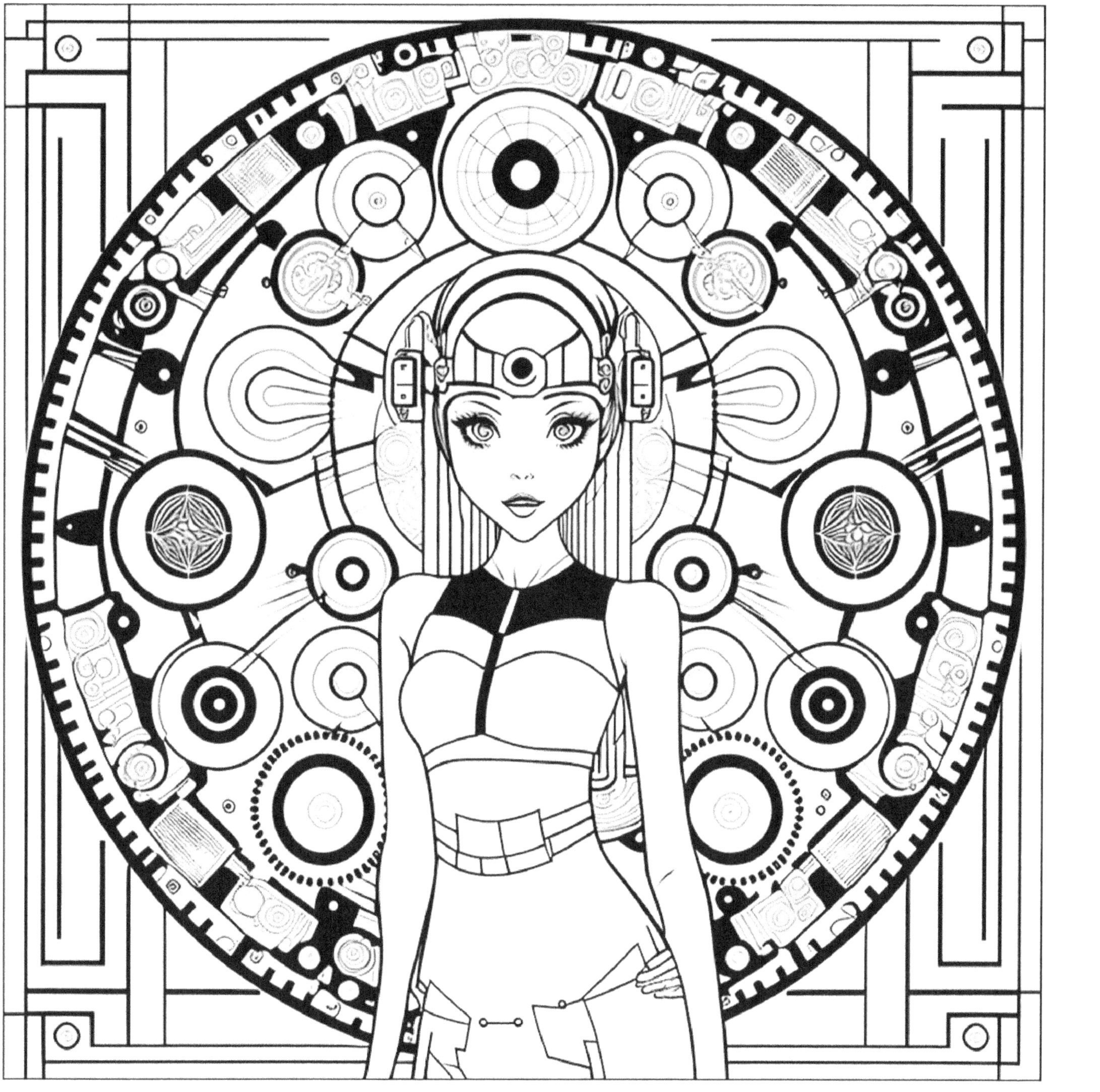

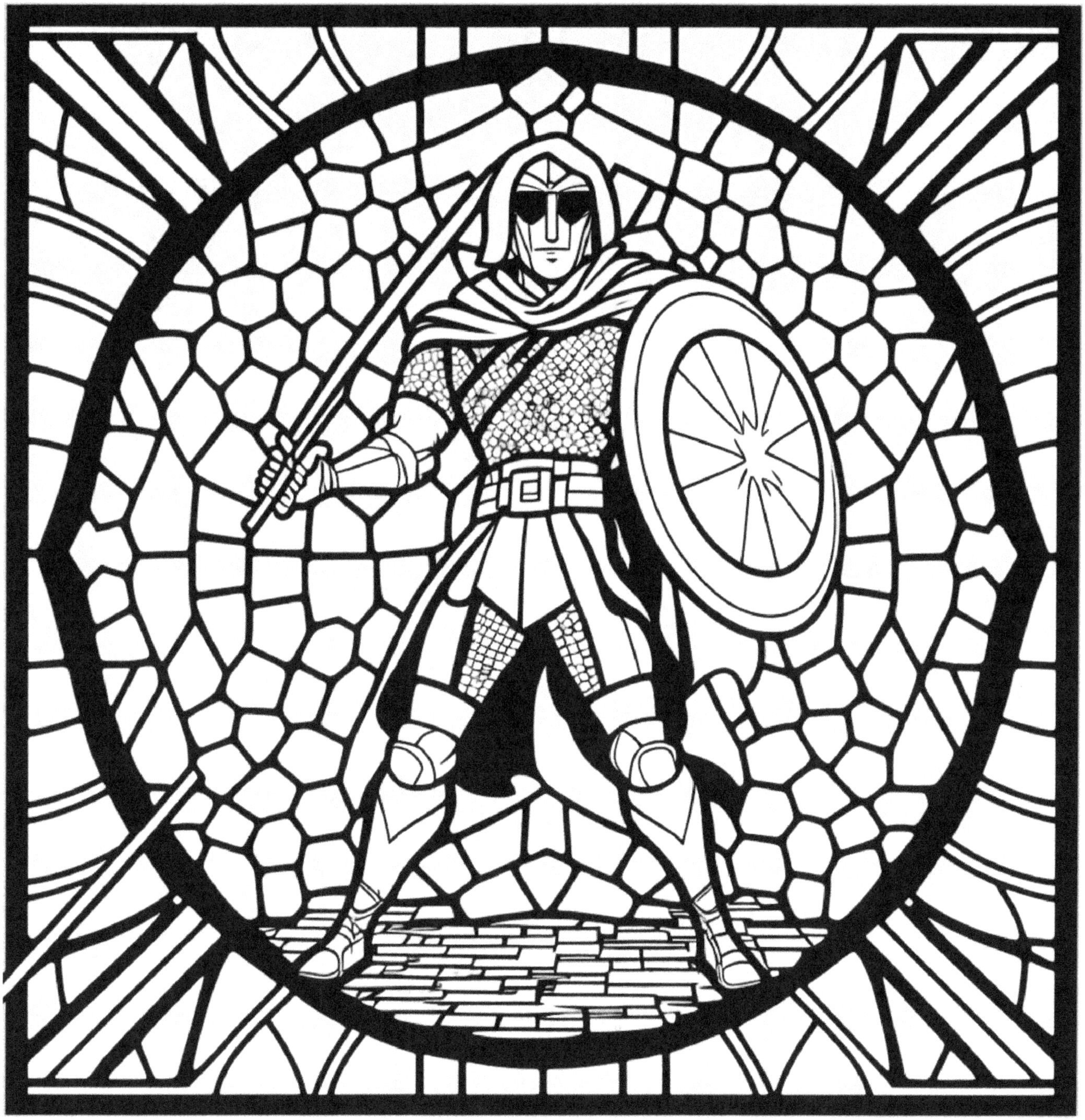

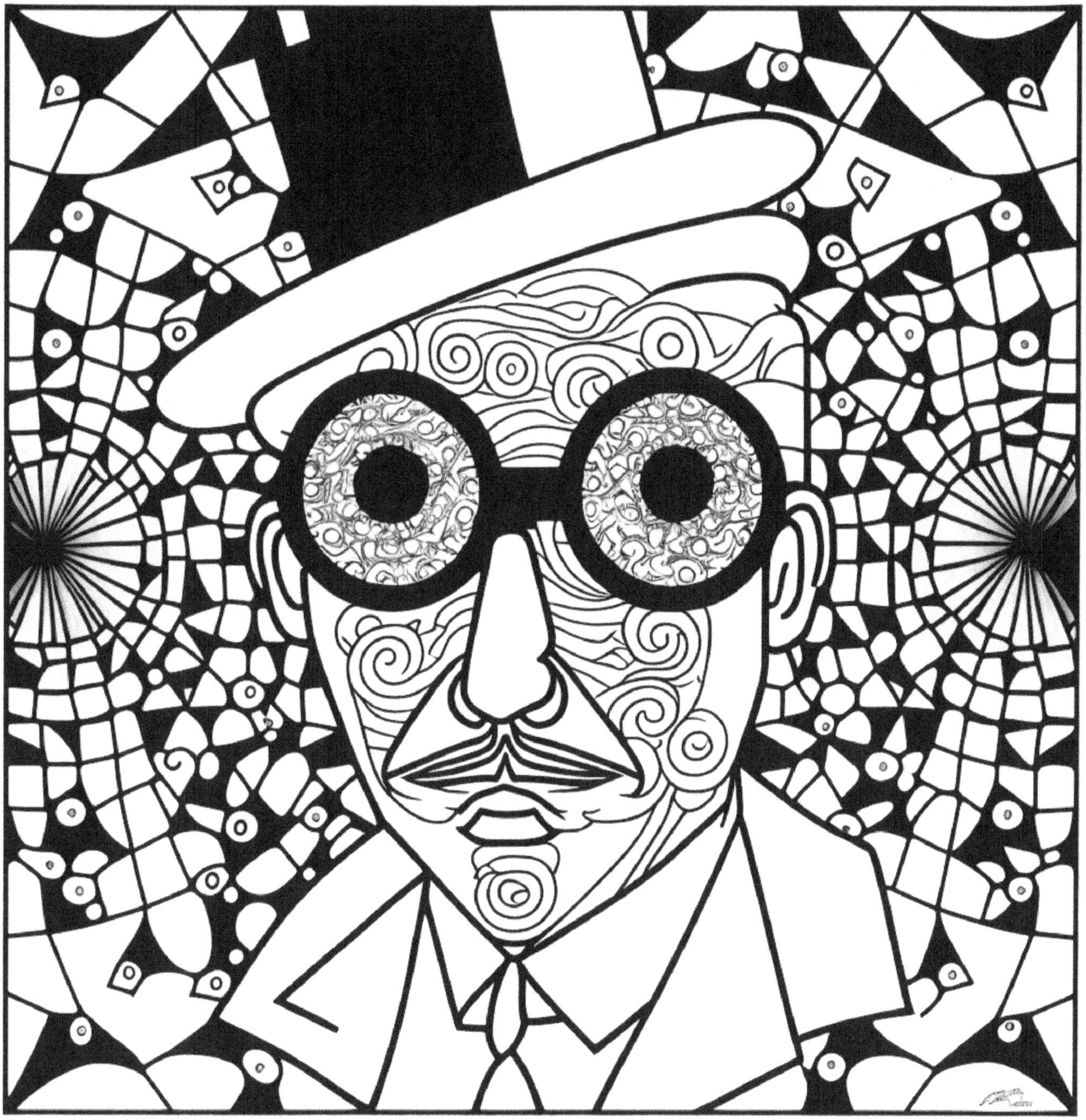

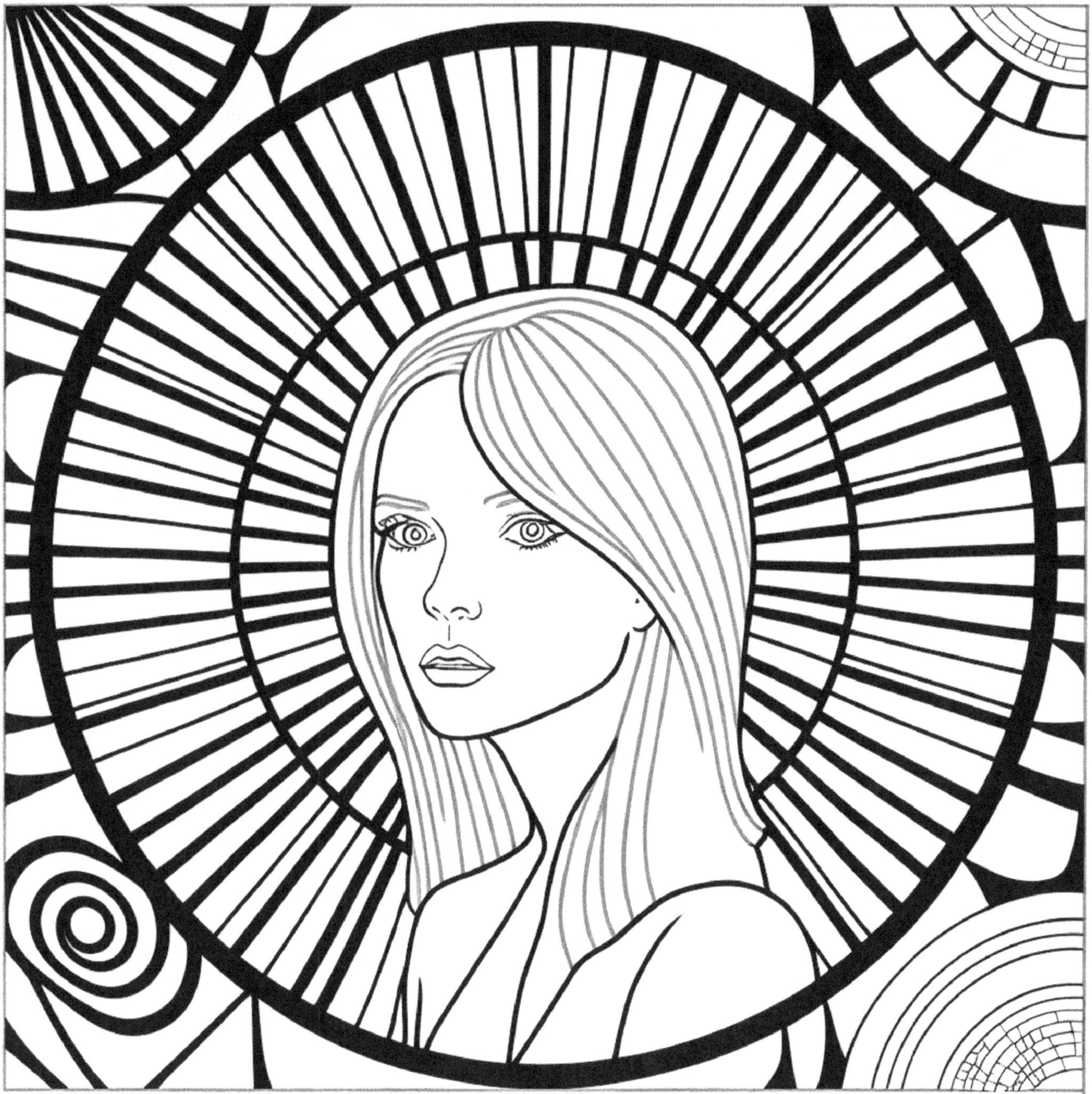

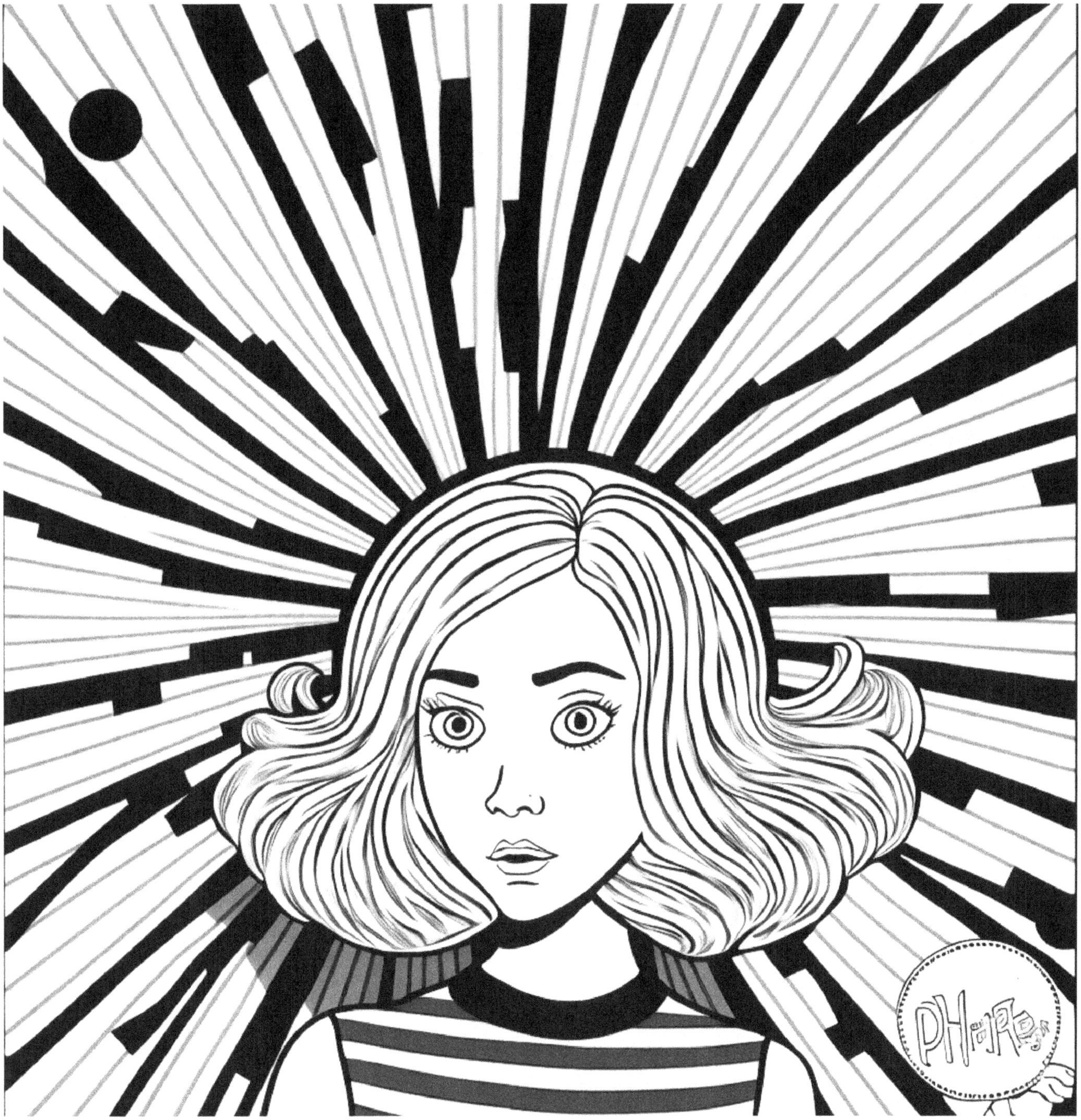

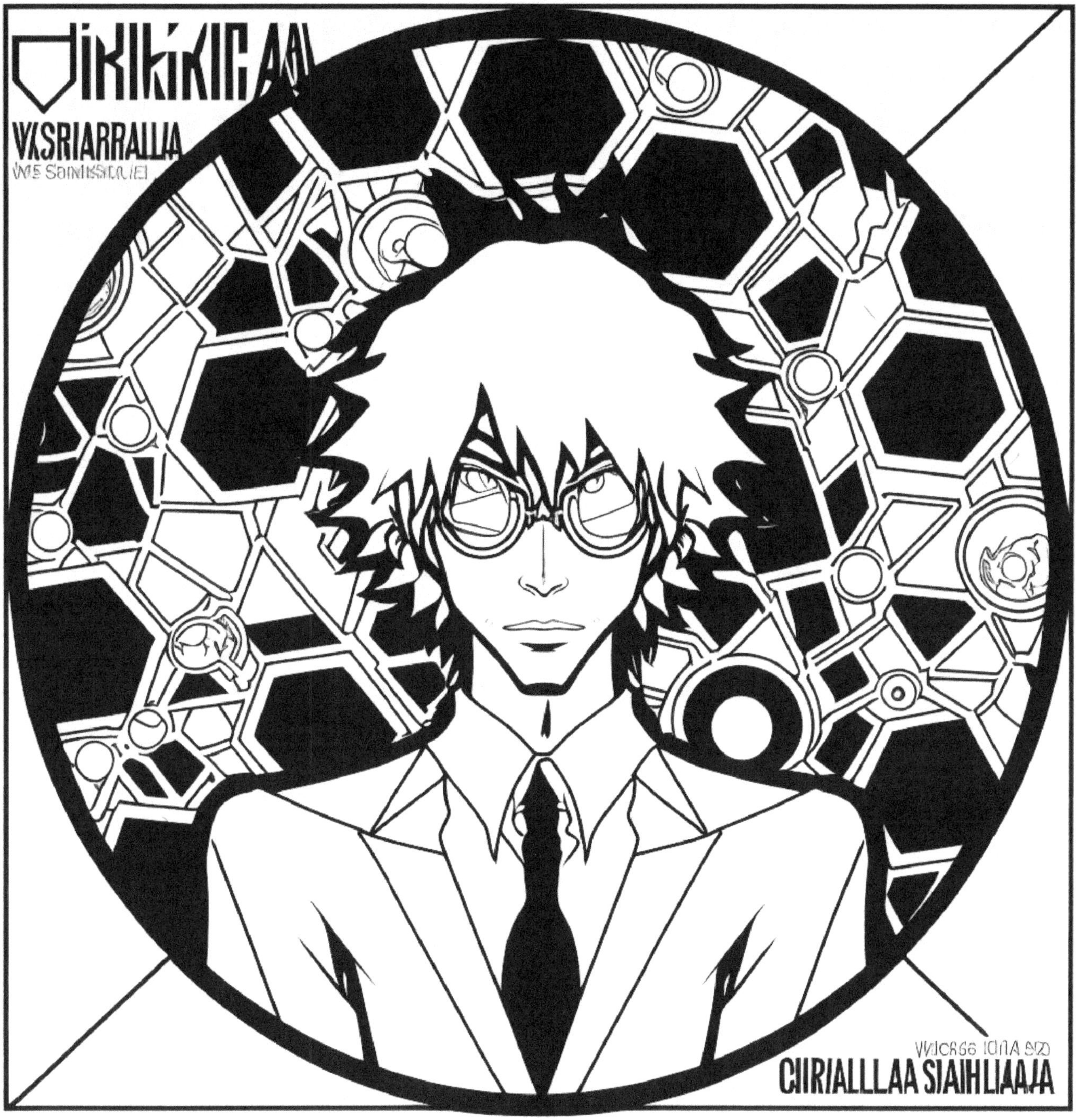

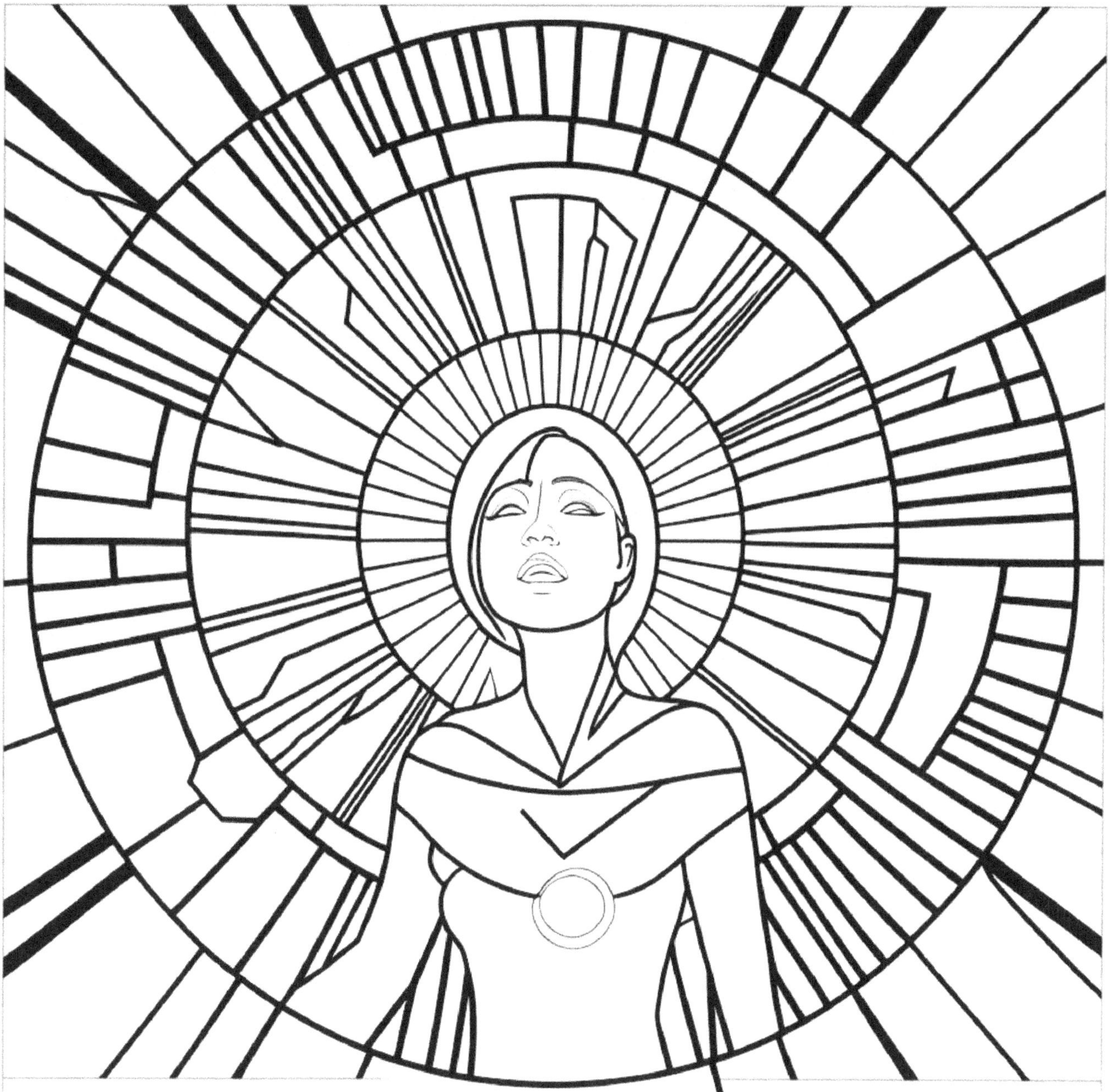

Pielny pteten vkalterles nassefiguis od ofro tredal Gleon

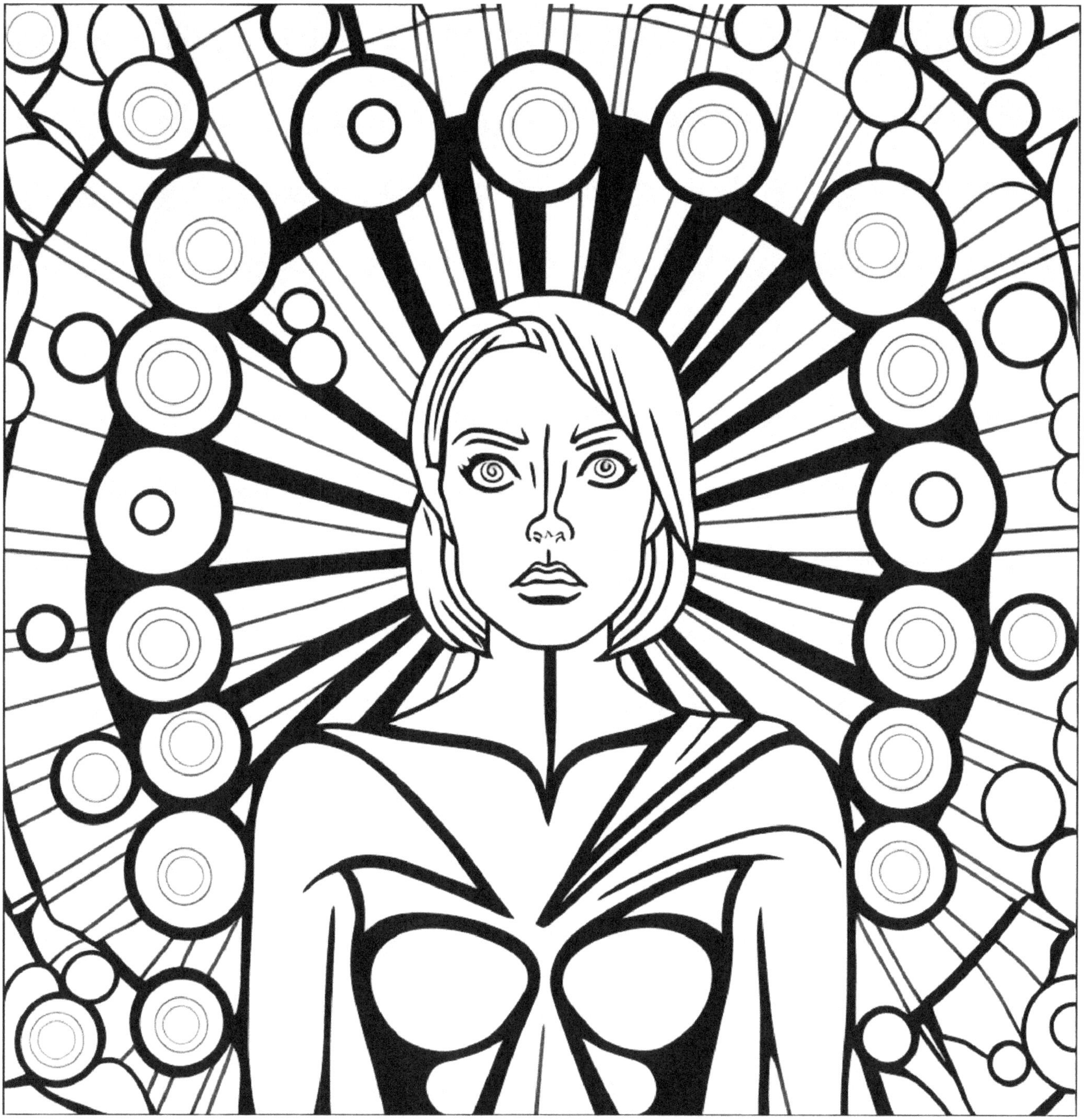

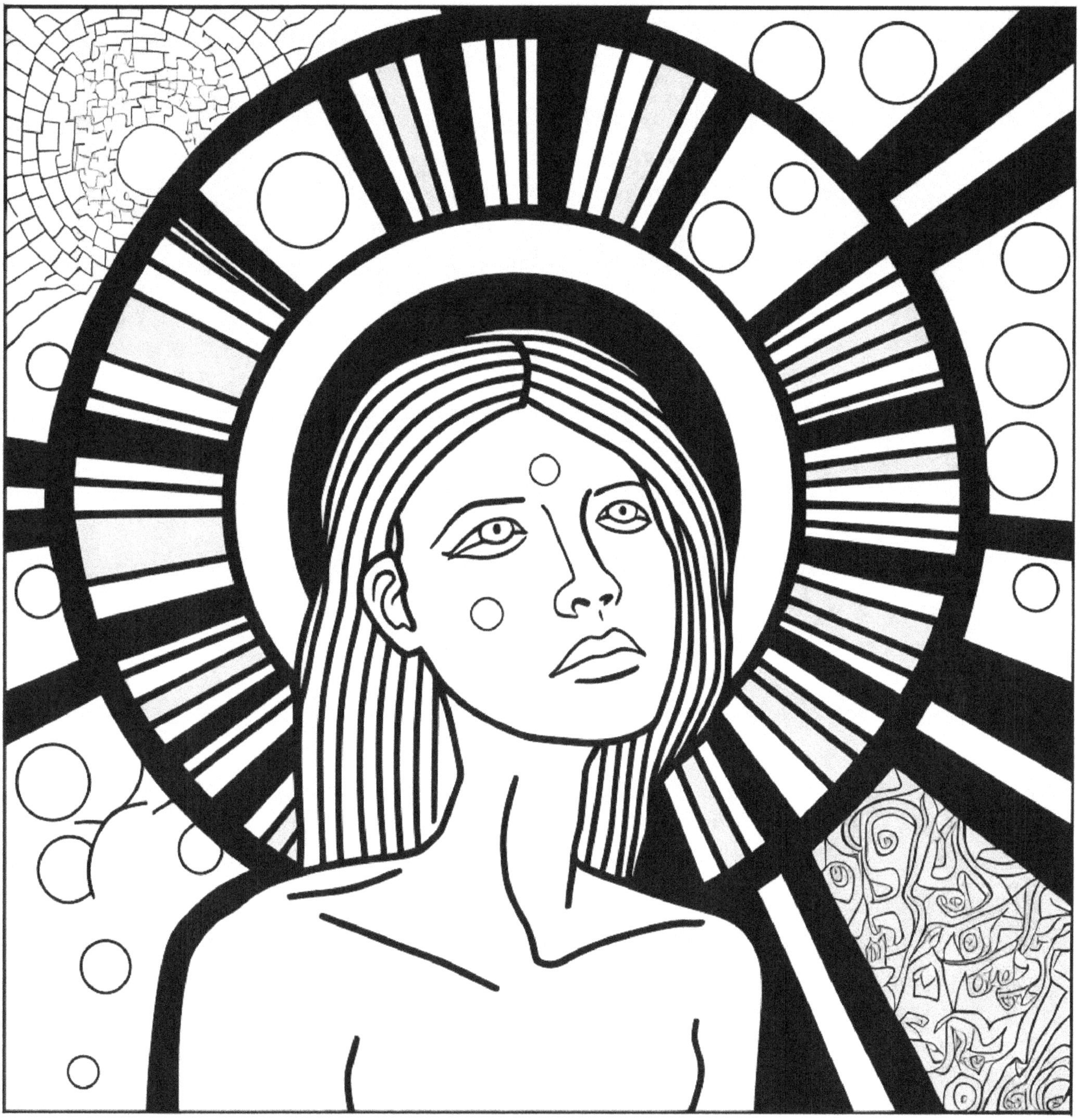

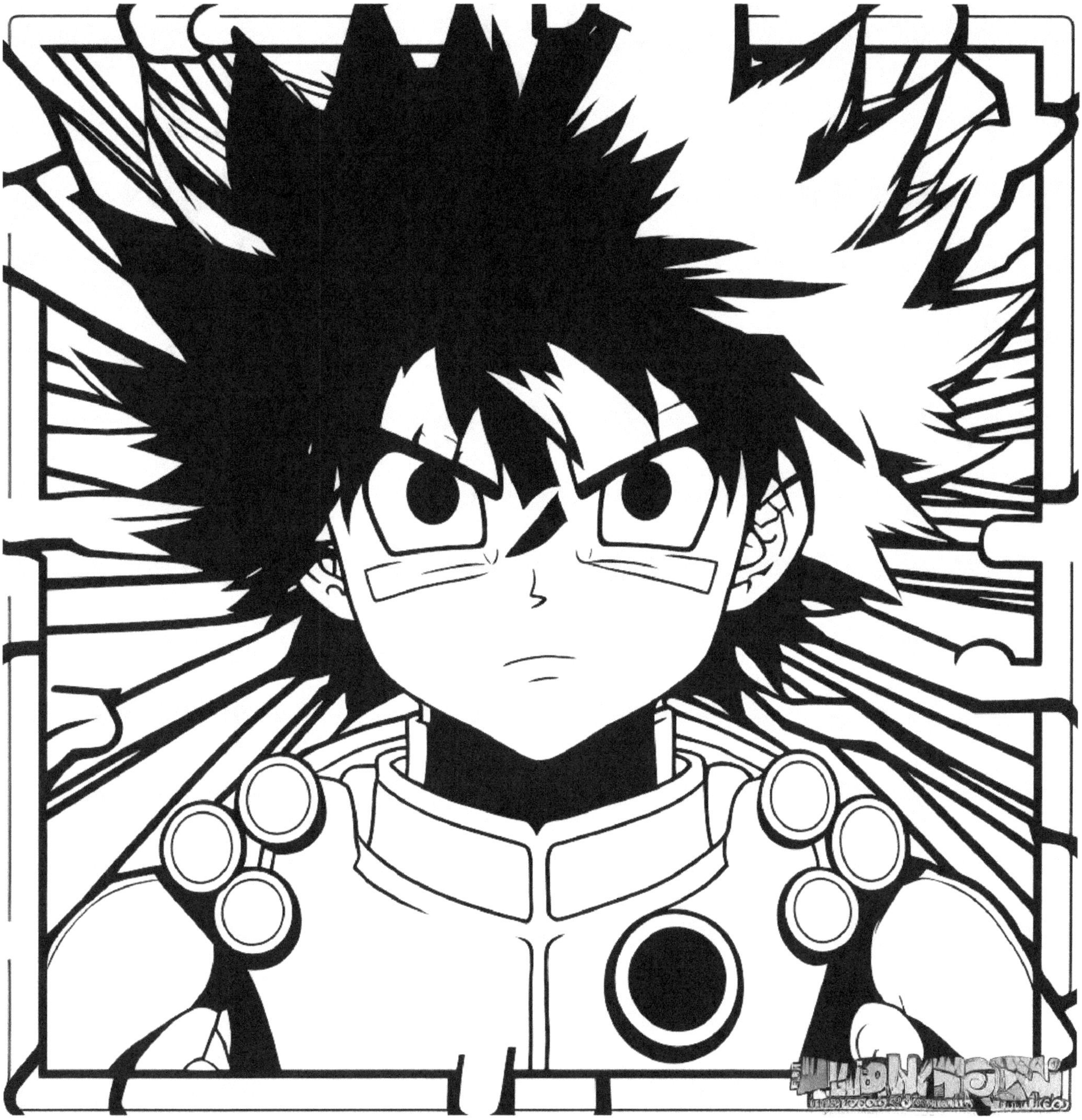

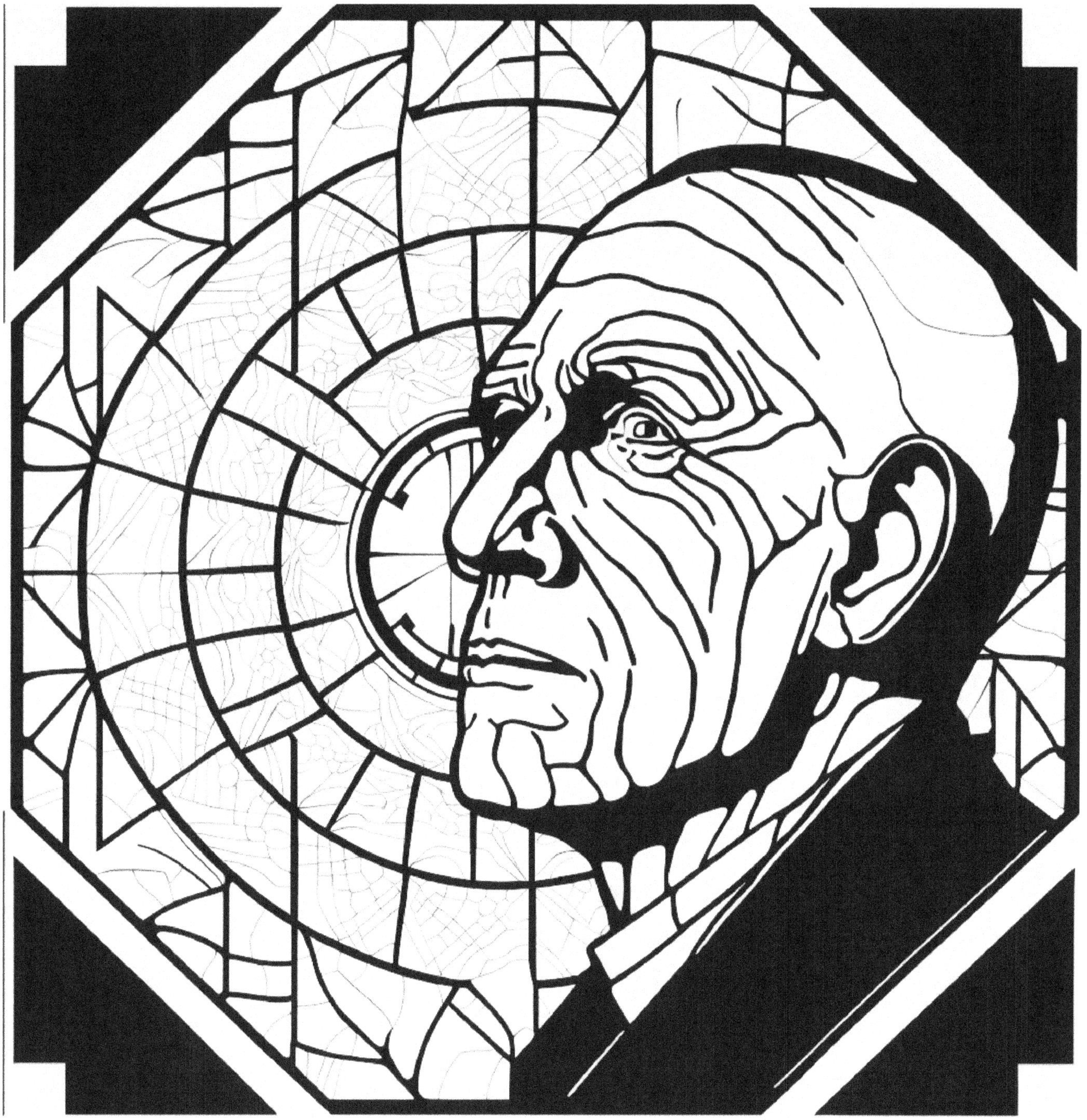

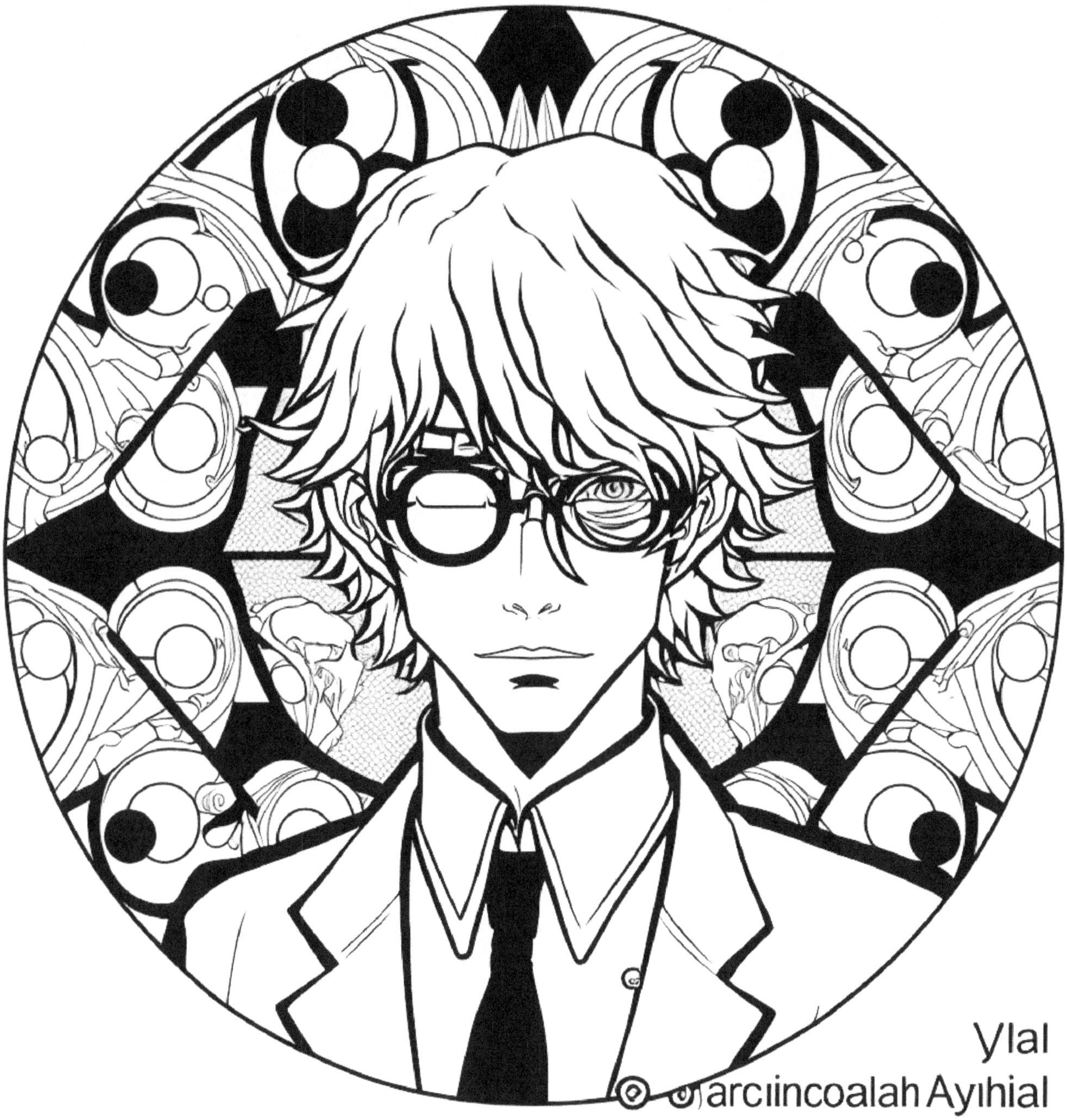
Ylal
arciincoalah Ayihial

www.ingramcontent.com/pod-product-compliance
Lightning Source LLC
Chambersburg PA
CBHW080107010626
45794CB00015B/3300
9798868051715